Places of Refuge

Wildlife refuges preserve the natural beauty of the land and provide sanctuary for its wild inhabitants.

Dorothy Hinshaw Patent

Places of Refuge
OUR NATIONAL WILDLIFE REFUGE SYSTEM

✦ ✦ ✦

—— Photographs by ——
William Muñoz

CLARION BOOKS ✦ NEW YORK

The author and photographer wish to thank all the employees of the U.S. Fish and Wildlife Service who helped us with this project; it would not have been possible without them. Special thanks go to Nancy Marx, who helped the author in many ways by providing information and giving advice.

Clarion Books
a Houghton Mifflin Company imprint
215 Park Avenue South, New York, NY 10003
Text copyright © 1992 by Dorothy Hinshaw Patent
Photographs copyright © 1992 by William Muñoz

Printed in Hong Kong

Library of Congress Cataloging-in-Publication Data
Patent, Dorothy Hinshaw.
Places of refuge : our national wildlife refuge system /
by Dorothy Hinshaw Patent ; photographs by William Muñoz.
p.   cm.
Includes index.
Summary: Examines some of the popular wildlife refuges,
in such states as Texas, North Dakota, and California, and
focuses on the different methods used to help maintain a
natural balance there.
ISBN 0-89919-846-5
1. Wildlife refuges—United States—Juvenile literature.
2. National parks and reserves—United States—Juvenile literature.
3. U.S. Fish and Wildlife Service—Juvenile literature.   [1. Wildlife refuges.
2. National parks and reserves.   3. Wildlife conservation.]
I. Muñoz, William, ill.   II. Title.
QL84.2.P38   1992
333.95′0973—dc20
91-29273
CIP
AC

I M S 10 9 8 7 6 5 4 3 2 1

*F*or the photographer's brother, Dick Muñoz,
and his wonderful family—Ann, Mark, and Danny—
and to all the other dedicated people who work
to preserve our wildlife and its habitat.

Rabbit taking shelter in a wildlife refuge.

Canada goose.

Contents

•1•

WHAT IS A REFUGE? 11

•2•

REFUGE PORTRAITS 27

•3•

MANAGING FOR WILDLIFE 45

•4•

PROBLEMS WITH REFUGES 51

•5•

REFUGES IN THE FUTURE 69

Where to Write for More Information 77

Index 79

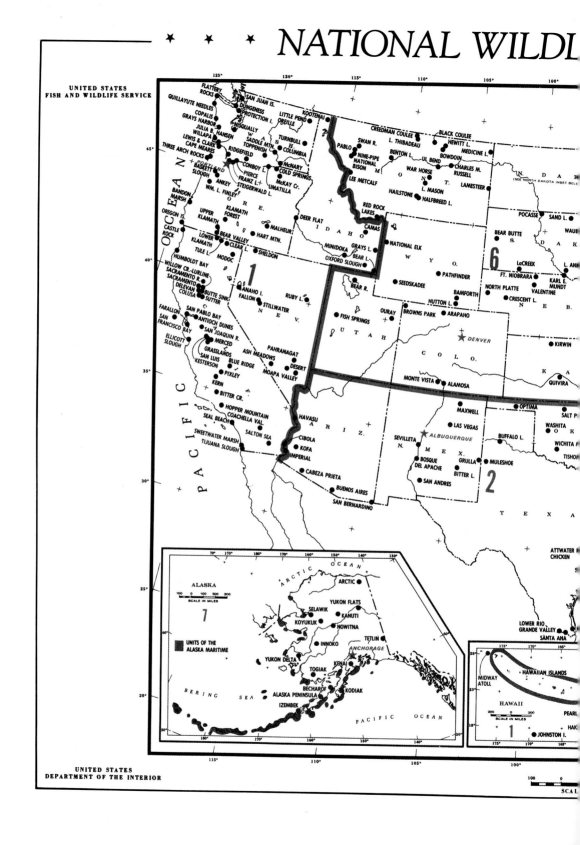

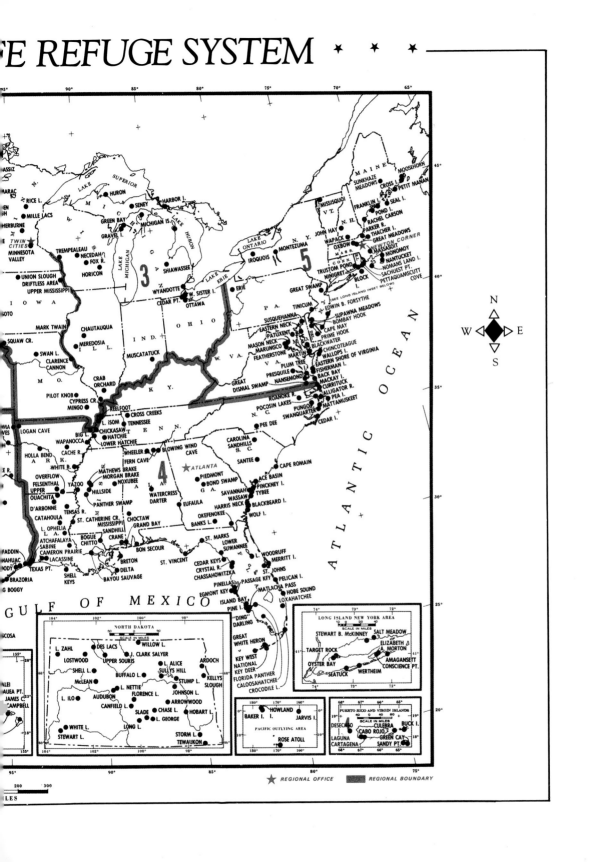

N
W ◆ E
S

REGIONAL OFFICE ★   REGIONAL BOUNDARY ■

What Is a Refuge?

Almost every day it's on the news—another species is endangered, or a new battle has begun to stop the destruction of a forest or a marsh that is home to a variety of animals. Are there any places left in our country where wild creatures can live in habitat that is renewed, not destroyed?

The National Wildlife Refuge System was started in 1903 to provide just such places—homes for wildlife. President Theodore Roosevelt was concerned that the fashion craze for feathers used in hats would wipe out beautiful native birds, such as the great egret. He set aside tiny three-acre Pelican Island in Florida as a protected place where birds could raise their families undisturbed by humans. Soon, two other bird refuges were established.

The National Bison Range is one of the oldest wildlife refuges.

Birds like the roseate spoonbill (top) and cattle egrets (bottom) nest on wildlife refuges like McFadden, in Texas.

Birds weren't the only animals threatened with extinction early in the twentieth century—so were large native mammals. In 1905, the Wichita Mountains National Wildlife Refuge in Oklahoma was set aside as a home for bison, followed in 1908 by the National Bison Range in Montana. Refuges for elk and pronghorn antelope soon followed. The National Wildlife Refuge System was on its way to becoming established as the world's most unique system of lands and waters set aside to enhance wildlife and benefit the public.

More Land for Animals

By 1934, there were 120 refuges in the System, which is managed by the U.S. Fish and Wildlife Service. That year, the Duck Stamp Law gave the System a big boost. Hunters were

The National Bison Range was established as a safe home for bison, also called buffalo.

concerned that wetlands—the marshes and ponds that ducks and geese need for breeding and as migration stopovers—were being drained, filled, and converted into farm land and home sites. The Duck Stamp Law required all hunters of waterfowl—ducks, swans, and geese—to pay a dollar for a special duck stamp when they bought their hunting licenses. The money collected was used to buy and protect wetlands.

Most wildlife refuges provide nesting areas for mallard ducks and other waterfowl.

The first year, $635,000 was raised. The money went a long way in those days. In 1940, when duck stamp sales topped a million dollars, wetlands in some areas were going for only a dollar an acre. Such bargain prices helped to dramatically increase the number of refuges—180 new refuges came into being between 1934 and 1941. Today, land is much more expensive and hunters pay $15.00 for a duck stamp. Duck stamps bring in a significant amount of money for buying and protecting habitat—more than $20 million in 1990.

Refuges provide critical wetland habitat for waterfowl and other species. Most refuges are concentrated along four major routes used by migrating waterfowl—the Atlantic, Mississippi, Central, and Pacific flyways. By far the largest number of protected acres in the system—over 77 million—lie in Alaska, where millions of birds fly to nest and raise their families.

The tradition of saving habitats for rare and endangered species has also continued. A variety of refuges has been set aside for this purpose. Aransas, in Texas, protects the endangered whooping crane during the winter months; Antioch

Squaw Creek National Wildlife Refuge provides a stopover place for waterfowl along the Central and Mississippi flyways.

Whooping cranes at Aransas National Wildlife Refuge.

Dunes in California provides a home for two endangered plants and an endangered butterfly. Other refuges protect different species in danger of extinction.

Recently, the Refuge System has placed greater emphasis on managing for biological diversity. Instead of concentrating on waterfowl habitat or on rescuing endangered species, preserving diversity means taking into consideration the needs of all the different kinds of plants and animals on a refuge.

The Variety of Refuges

Today, about 470 National Wildlife Refuges covering more than 91 million acres dot the land of every state in the United States, as well as Puerto Rico, American Samoa, and the U.S.

Virgin Islands. New areas are added every year. Refuges represent every type of habitat, from desert so dry only an inch of rain falls in a year to rainforests where hardly a day passes without a shower or two. The Salton Sea National Wildlife Refuge in California is 226 feet below sea level, while the mountains in Desert National Wildlife Range in Nevada climb to over 9,000 feet. The wind chill at Des Lacs National Wildlife Refuge in North Dakota can reach $-105°F$, while Havasu National Wildlife Refuge, which straddles the Arizona-California Border, can have more than a hundred days a year of temperatures over 100°F.

Wildlife refuges protect all sorts of habitats, including swamps like Okefenokee National Wildlife Refuge in Georgia.

Some refuges, like Kenai in Alaska, provide safe homes for marine animals like these sea lions. Photo by Dorothy H. Patent.

Each refuge has its own legal purpose—preserving the habitat for an endangered species or the breeding grounds for waterfowl, for example. Refuge lands are managed as much as possible to further these purposes. The goal of the System is not primarily to preserve habitat in its original state, but rather to restore and enhance the land to benefit wildlife. This goal is often misunderstood by the public. The aim is healthy populations of wildlife, not survival of each individual of the species. Overpopulated species like deer may be hunted on refuges; water may be dammed to create marshes; or visitors may be forbidden to enter areas critical to breeding of endangered species, all with the intent of aiding wildlife populations.

The broad goals of the Refuge System also include providing "recreational activities oriented toward wildlife" for humans. Thus, many refuges give people a chance to enjoy

Prairie pothole habitat like that found in Agassiz National Wildlife Refuge in Minnesota is very important for waterfowl reproduction.

Deer, like the mule deer at Bosque del Apache National Wildlife Refuge in New Mexico, are common on many refuges.

outdoor activities such as hiking, auto touring, and bird watching. In addition, a number of refuges, like the San Francisco Bay National Wildlife Refuge in California and Tinicum National Environmental Center near Philadelphia, Pennsylvania, emphasize environmental education. Volunteers and employees lead nature hikes, and school children come to learn about the wildlife that lives near their homes.

Sometimes, human recreation on refuges, such as running power boats, disturbs wildlife. About 38 percent of refuges allow sport hunting of certain birds and big game animals. In addition to recreation, some refuges are sites of economic uses such as grazing, logging, and mining. Others are locations for military activities, such as bombing practice. All these activities carry the risk of harming wildlife. The U.S. Fish and Wildlife Service is continually reviewing these activities to assess the potential impacts on wildlife populations.

*Some refuges, like Kilauea Point National Wildlife Refuge in Hawaii,
provide extensive environmental education as well as wildlife viewing.
Photo by Dorothy H. Patent.*

*There's life underwater at refuges, as these visitors are learning.
Courtesy U.S. Fish and Wildlife Service.*

Tinicum National Environmental Center is within sight of Philadelphia's skyscrapers. Courtesy U.S. Fish and Wildlife Service; photo by Stroup.

Kinds of Public Lands

There are many kinds of public lands in the United States, each with its own purposes and allowed uses. National parks, managed by the National Park Service, are probably the most familiar type. In a national park, the plants and animals are left alone as much as possible to live out their lives naturally. While people can camp, fish, and hike in national parks, activities such as hunting, mining, and logging are not allowed.

National forests, managed by the U.S. Forest Service, are lands set aside for "multiple use." Logging, mining, hiking, camping, and hunting are all permitted in national forests. In

Parks like Glacier National Park in Montana also provide homes for a variety of wildlife, like this mountain goat.

Logging is common in national forests—here you can see clearcuts and logging roads in the Bitterroot National Forest in Montana. Photo by Dorothy H. Patent.

many areas, people who wish to cut down trees argue with others who want to preserve wildlife homes and provide quiet places for hiking and camping.

The Bureau of Land Management controls the National Resource Lands, which are largely in dry western states, where mining and livestock grazing, as well as recreation, are allowed. In addition, the Department of Defense has land in different states that it uses for bases and training, and the Bureau of Reclamation controls land that provides irrigation water for western farmers.

Wilderness areas can be parts of any public lands that are set aside to remain as natural as possible. A wilderness can

Here, water from the Rio Grande River is diverted for Bosque del Apache National Wildlife Refuge. Refuges often have to share precious resources, such as water, with private interests, such as agriculture.

have no roads, and no motorized vehicles are allowed. Buildings are also forbidden.

In addition to the public lands owned by the federal government, states have their own parks, forests, and preserves, each controlled by state laws. Counties and cities also operate parks, some of which provide wildlife habitat.

As the human population of our country grows, more and more demand is made on public lands. Mining companies, loggers, and other special interest groups increasingly lobby for permission to carry out their activities. Refuges feel the pressure strongly because they cover so much land and because they have allowed so many uses in the past. But this is changing. As the twenty-first century approaches, along with the System's one hundredth birthday in 2003, clashes among users of refuges become more and more painfully obvious. The Refuge System management is working to eliminate activities that can harm wildlife populations, and conservation organizations such as Defenders of Wildlife and The Wilderness Society are demanding that the needs of wildlife on our refuges be put before the activities and pleasures of humans.

·2·

Refuge Portraits

J ust what are you likely to find if you visit a wildlife refuge? Some, like the Farallon National Wildlife Refuge, an island of rock and boulders off the California coast, are completely closed to visitors. Others may provide little or nothing in the way of facilities for human visitors. But a large number of refuges welcome people who are interested in wildlife. They have visitors' centers explaining the refuges' purposes and management activities and pointing out what wildlife lives there. They also have foot trails and/or auto tour drives to encourage exploring.

Bosque del Apache National Wildlife Refuge

Established in 1939 "as a refuge and breeding grounds for waterfowl and other wildlife," Bosque del Apache National

(Overleaf) Sunrise at Bosque del Apache National Wildlife Refuge shows birds roosting safely in the water.

Sandhill cranes.

Wildlife Refuge has traditionally been a haven for endangered species. Bosque lies in New Mexico, along the Rio Grande River. An original goal at Bosque was protecting the then-endangered greater sandhill crane. Now these birds have increased so that they are no longer threatened with extinction. Today, the endangered bald eagle and peregrine falcon also find homes on the refuge.

Bosque has been involved in an unusual experiment designed to help save the endangered whooping crane. For a number of years, whooping crane eggs were placed in the nests of sandhill cranes at Grays Lake National Wildlife Refuge in Idaho. The sandhills raised the chicks as their own, and the whooping cranes flew with their foster parents to Bosque for the winter. The egg transplanting has now ended, but about a dozen whooping cranes still spend the winters in New Mexico with the sandhills.

During the wintertime, tens of thousands of birds live at Bosque, especially snow geese, ducks, and sandhill cranes. Bird watchers and wildlife photographers flock to the refuge during the winter months along with the birds, to see them and to take pictures.

Bosque is home to wildlife year around. Wild turkeys, coyotes, mule deer, porcupines, roadrunners—altogether, 295 different kinds of birds and 400 mammal species live there, most of them staying all year. The setting is beautiful, with

Mallard ducks are among the species that spend the winter at Bosque.

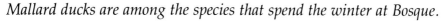

Cranes fly across the sunset at Bosque.

calm pond waters reflecting sculptured brown hills and spectacular sunsets.

The habitat at Bosque is managed to benefit wildlife. During the winter, water is pumped from irrigation canals and underground wells to form ponds and marshes where the migrating waterfowl can feed and rest. Only a few ponds are left during the summer. The others are drained, and the water is used for crop irrigation on nearby farms. Parts of the refuge are leased to farmers, who are required to leave a third of their crops for the wildlife in payment for use of the land.

Some hunting is allowed on Bosque. For example, each November, a special eight-day snow goose hunt is held. Since snow geese are white with black wing markings, like whooping cranes, required classes teach hunters how to tell one bird on the wing from another, and law enforcement is strict.

Cape Romain National Wildlife Refuge

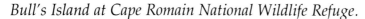

Cape Romain National Wildlife Refuge, along the Atlantic coast in South Carolina, is an important stopover for many migrating birds and a wintering area for others. The refuge consists mostly of offshore islands. The largest, Bull's Island,

Bull's Island at Cape Romain National Wildlife Refuge.

is wooded and in recent years has been the site for the release of endangered red wolves. Bull's Island is also home to dozens of bird species, despite tremendous damage from Hurricane Hugo in 1989.

Cape Romain provides rookeries—breeding areas used by large numbers of birds—for a variety of species, including the brown pelican, a species recovering from the threat of extinction. As many as 3,000 pairs of pelicans nest at Cape Romain each year.

Brown pelican rookery at Cape Romain.

A female loggerhead sea turtle digs her nest on Cape Romain National Wildlife Refuge.

The refuge is also an important nesting site for the endangered loggerhead sea turtle. From late May through early August, female turtles come out of the ocean at night and struggle across the sand to find places for their nests. Each female digs a deep hole in the sand using her front flippers. Then she turns around and lays her eggs in the hole, covering them with sand when she is finished.

Over the years, storms have washed away much of the sand from the turtle nesting beaches, so the nests can become swamped by the sea. Raccoons also raid them. To help the turtles survive, refuge personnel search the beaches for nests and move the eggs to protected pens on higher ground. When the young turtles are ready to hatch, employees spend the night on the island, releasing the hatchlings at the crest of the beach so the youngsters can find their way into the water.

San Francisco Bay National Wildlife Refuge

The San Francisco Bay National Wildlife Refuge was established in 1972. It is one of the largest urban refuges in the

San Francisco Bay National Wildlife Refuge protects important habitat for wildlife along the San Francisco Bay coastline.

The bay mudflats provide feeding areas for a variety of shorebirds.

System. It protects wildlife habitat around the edges of the south portion of San Francisco Bay. The shores of the bay have been so developed that 90 percent of the wetlands are gone. The refuge is therefore vitally important to protecting a part of what little is left.

These wetlands are home to many plants and animals. Dark green pickleweed grows across the flats, and birds such as avocets and sandpipers probe into the black, muddy shore. It may not be a spectacular sight, but much more is going on than can be seen easily. Two endangered species, the salt marsh harvest mouse and the California clapper rail, make their homes here. Dozens of kinds of tiny creatures, including microscopic life, insects, worms, and shellfish, live in the mud. One handful of mud can contain as many as 40,000 such beings, providing a vital link in the food web of the bay. Crabs, shrimp, oysters, and food fish such as halibut depend on this food web, as do many species of birds.

During the fall and winter, millions of ducks and shore-

Dick Muñoz gives instruction to volunteers who will help in the San Francisco Bay National Wildlife Refuge environmental education programs.

birds converge on the bay from Canada, Alaska, and the Pacific Northwest, and thousands of them make their homes in the San Francisco Bay National Wildlife Refuge. Half of the canvasback ducks on the west coast rely on San Francisco Bay for their survival.

Because it is located in a major metropolitan area with millions of residents, the San Francisco Bay National Wildlife Refuge has tens of thousands of visitors each year. Environmental education is part of its purpose; films, walks led by naturalists, and weekend lectures help teach visitors what to look for and how to appreciate their special refuge.

A refuge employee points out things to look for at Iroquois National Wildlife Refuge in New York. Courtesy U.S. Fish and Wildlife Service; photo by Lawrence Smith.

Aransas National Wildlife Refuge in springtime.

· 3 ·

Managing for Wildlife

Running a wildlife refuge takes a lot of work. Because so little of the land in the United States remains undeveloped, those wildlands that remain are used heavily by wild creatures. The people who work on the refuges do their best to provide good habitats for the plants and animals that depend on them for homes.

Helping Endangered Species

Antioch Dunes National Wildlife Refuge in northern California is tiny, only 67 acres. Yet it is home to three endangered species found nowhere else. The Antioch dunes are a very special habitat. They were once connected to inland deserts rather than to coastal sand dunes, so the plants and animals that lived there were more closely related to desert than to coastal species.

Lange's metalmark butterfly.

The dunes probably once covered about 500 acres. But, starting in the 1880s, sand was mined from the dunes, destroying most of them. Industrial development, agriculture, and home building eliminated almost all the rest. The only reason any dunes remain is that the Pacific Gas and Electric Company happened to install electric transmission lines in the area in 1909 and 1927. The only dune habitat left is under those lines. Now the company works together with U.S. Fish and Wildlife Service personnel to protect the dunes and their plants and animals.

Lange's metalmark is a pretty little endangered butterfly that relies on buckwheat growing on the refuge. The adult butterflies feed on nectar from the blossoms, and the females lay their eggs on the leaves. Buckwheat is the only plant the caterpillars will eat. To help the butterfly survive, the forty-acre area where the buckwheat is concentrated is closed to the public. Buckwheat seeds are collected and planted to increase the food supply available to the butterflies.

The Contra Costa wallflower.

Antioch Dunes evening primrose.

On the refuge, the Contra Costa wallflower blooms in the spring, producing a tall stalk decorated by bright yellow flowers. The Antioch Dunes evening primrose produces large, pretty white flowers tinged with pink from March through July. The flowers open in the evening and close again by mid-morning. Both these endangered plants live only on the refuge, thriving in the open sandy areas of the dunes.

Helping Animals Breed

The loss of habitat for wildlife has meant fewer and fewer suitable places for breeding, especially for birds. Many wildlife refuges help birds by providing them with places to nest.

Bluebirds normally rely on holes in trees for nesting. But the older trees that are more likely to have nesting holes are becoming scarce. Fortunately, bluebirds will also nest in a box nailed to a tree, if it is the right size and shape. Bluebird boxes on refuges allow the birds to raise their families successfully.

In recent years, the numbers of many species of ducks in the United States have been decreasing at an alarming rate.

Primrose plants are transplanted to help increase their abundance on the refuge.

A male mountain bluebird.

The prairie pothole region of North America, which stretches from South Dakota through eastern Montana and North Dakota into Canada, once produced 30 million ducks each year. By the early 1980s, that number was down to less than 20 million. One reason for the decrease is drought—not enough rain to fill the ponds, potholes, and marshes the birds need for successful breeding. The major reason, however, is continued loss of wetlands through draining for farming and development.

As private wetlands decrease, public ones such as wildlife

Cattails are used as nesting areas by yellow-headed blackbirds.

Digging channels to provide duck breeding habitat at Lee Metcalf National Wildlife Refuge in Montana.

refuges become more and more critical to the continued survival of waterfowl. Refuge habitat can be modified to increase duck breeding. A thick growth of cattails in marshes provides good breeding areas for blackbirds and marsh wrens, but not for ducks. Duck breeding habitat can be restored by digging channels through the marshes. Since a male mallard makes his breeding territory as far as he can see along the water, the channels are dug in zigzags so more ducks can breed in the area.

While some ducks, such as mallards, mate in the wetlands, the females build their nests away from the water, protected

A pair of mallards at Lee Metcalf National Wildlife Refuge.

During the wintertime, when water in the refuge is low, an artificial nesting site for Canada geese is constructed at Ninepipe National Wildlife Refuge in Montana.

by tall grasses or bushes. For them, preserving such uplands adjacent to the water is very important. Other species of waterfowl, like Canada geese, prefer to build their nests on islands or clumps of plants in the water. The number of good nesting sites for such birds can be increased by building artificial islands in the water.

·4·

Problems with Refuges

*B*ecause of the pressure of our ever-growing human population, our National Wildlife Refuges have become very controversial places in areas where the needs of nature and humans conflict. Solutions to these problems need to be found, since our refuges are critical to the survival of North American wildlife. Conservation groups and the U.S. Fish and Wildlife Service are working hard to find ways to protect refuges in our modern crowded world.

Refuges and Recreation

Our National Wildlife Refuges provide important places for recreation for many people. Unfortunately, human recreational activities can cause problems for wildlife. Some animals, like ground squirrels and mule deer, quickly adapt to

Ninepipe National Wildlife Refuge in Montana.

humans and are not particularly bothered by them. But others, such as bald eagles, are very sensitive to disturbance and have difficulty raising young if people are around too much of the time. For this reason, many refuges have only part of their land open to the public, leaving areas where native plants and animals can live relatively undisturbed.

Some kinds of recreation can be harmful to the environment and, therefore, to wild things. Nine percent of refuges allow off-road vehicles, which can tear up the ground badly, killing plants and encouraging erosion. The vehicles also make noise that disturbs wildlife. Power boats can injure slow-moving animals such as the endangered manatee in Florida. Horses used for riding (allowed on 27 percent of refuges in 1989) cut up the ground with their hooves and spread weed seeds through their manure.

Sometimes just the sheer numbers of people using a refuge

Chipmunks and many other animals can become used to human visitors at refuges, but some animals are not so adaptable.

Sunrise at Chincoteague National Wildlife Refuge. Courtesy U.S. Fish and Wildlife Service; photo by Joe Knecht.

can be a problem. Chincoteague National Wildlife Refuge in Virginia is used by a million and a half beach-goers every year. Yet the refuge is a major breeding area for an endangered bird, the piping plover. During the 1980s, the sunbathers' presence was making it difficult for the birds to nest successfully. So, beginning in 1988, two-and-a-half miles of the beach were closed to people during the spring and summer to protect the plovers during their breeding season.

About a mile of public recreational beach remains, providing enough space for the sunbathers. Another mile-and-a-half of beach is reserved for off-road vehicle use, while several miles of wild beach are set aside for wildlife viewing.

To Hunt or Not to Hunt?

Hunting on wildlife refuges is a very controversial subject. The money from duck stamps bought by waterfowl hunters brings in millions of dollars each year for buying and conserving wetlands. But because the numbers of many duck species keep declining, some people think waterfowl should be left

Populations of the beautiful cinnamon teal are dropping.

alone on refuges. The impact of hunting on bird populations is questionable, since habitat loss is the major reason for reduced bird populations. Still, a number of hunters are concerned enough about the decline of waterfowl that they buy their duck stamp each year but refrain from hunting.

Some hunters who use refuges are learning ways to minimize negative effects. Birds are hunted with buckshot—small metal pellets that spread out from the end of the gun barrel, which increases the chances of hitting birds in flight. Until recently, most buckshot was made from lead. Leftover lead pellets sink to the marsh bottom and are eaten by water birds. Many birds eat enough lead to poison them, and they die. Bald eagles have become part of this death chain. They are poisoned by eating birds left behind by hunters as well as birds that have died from lead poisoning.

Hunters on refuges are now required to use steel shot. Some refuges give classes to teach hunters how steel shot differs from lead. Hunters are also instructed in other aspects of safe, unwasteful hunting. For example, demonstrations encourage them to use dogs to retrieve downed birds, reducing waste.

Deer can be a problem on wildlife refuges, just as they are in some suburban neighborhoods. Their main natural enemy, the wolf, is absent, so deer populations can grow fast. The deer feed on cover plants needed by the smaller wildlife, reducing their numbers. They eat young trees so that there are no growing trees to replace those that die. And if deer are allowed to continue to increase, they eventually consume the available food supply and die of starvation.

Since humans have eliminated most of the deer's preda-

A hunter practices with steel shot at Lee Metcalf National Wildlife Refuge.

A Labrador retriever demonstrates his retrieving ability at Lee Metcalf National Wildlife Refuge.

Deer populations need to be controlled at many refuges, since too many deer damage the habitat for other animals.

tors, we are responsible for solving the problems created by deer. When there are too many deer, they must be removed by people in some way. Just about every place has as many deer as it can support, which means the animals cannot be captured and released elsewhere. Besides, capturing deer is extremely difficult to do and is very stressful to them. The deer must be killed. The question is whether refuge personnel should shoot excess animals or whether sport hunting should be allowed.

Big-game hunting—which almost always means at least deer hunting—was allowed on 38 percent of refuges in 1989. But on the National Bison Range in western Montana, hunting is not permitted. Instead, excess deer are shot by refuge personnel and the meat is given to local schools for their hot lunch programs. Every year, some of the bison are auctioned off so that their numbers remain constant. When antelope became overpopulated, some were caught and moved across the river to land owned by the Confederated Salish and Kootenai Tribes of the Flathead Indian Reservation, where more antelope were wanted.

Not Enough Water, Not Enough Clean Water

Like people, animals need water to survive. Waterfowl are especially dependent on water for overwintering and for successful breeding. But as agriculture and human population increase, water becomes harder and harder to come by, and wildlife suffers as a result.

The situation is especially bad in California, where little rain has fallen in recent years and the human population continues to grow. Consequently, land and water available for waterfowl has decreased dramatically. Once there were 5 million acres of wetlands in the state. By the mid-1980s, the acreage had fallen to 300,000, and the number of overwintering birds had dropped to a fraction of what it was before.

The Central Valley of California was once a wildlife para-

Lee Metcalf National Wildlife Refuge provides winter habitat for many waterfowl.

dise. Although little or no rain falls there during the summer, streams and rivers draining the Sierra Nevada mountains to the east once created plenty of wetlands where millions of birds and other animals lived. Since the mid-1800s, almost 95

Pronghorn antelope are collected in net traps at the National Bison Range and then transferred to Indian lands across the river.

percent of those wetlands have been drained for agriculture. The rivers have been dammed and the streams turned into channels for distributing water to farms, businesses, and homes.

A number of wildlife refuges dot the Central Valley. But they have serious problems. During the 1980s, the federal government built ponds on part of Kesterton National Wildlife Refuge to evaporate water draining from farmlands. As the water evaporated, the concentration of poisonous chemicals, especially the element selenium, increased. The selenium killed birds and caused terrible deformities, such as twisted beaks, in the chicks raised on that part of the refuge. Now the ponds have been filled so the birds won't use the

When wetlands dry up, waterfowl lose their homes.

Waterfowl like these snow geese and Ross geese need open water for overwintering.

poisoned areas. But the problem of disposing of water that carries the agricultural waste chemicals remains.

Because of drought, the refuges in the Central Valley are in additional trouble. Their share of available water has been cut to the extent that there isn't enough water to last through the summer and fall until the rains start again. Meanwhile, the number of waterfowl that overwinter there keeps declining. In the 1940s, there were about 40 million birds. By the 1970s,

Marshlands like this one in the Central Valley of California are precious resources for wildlife. Courtesy U.S. Fish and Wildlife Service; photo by Dennis Peters.

the number was down to 10 or 12 million. By the early 1990s, the no more than 5 million birds left are crowded together on refuges with so little water they risk epidemics of disease that could reduce their numbers even further.

Dividing up water reserves is a very difficult problem. Agriculture is big business in California, and farmers get their water cheaply from the government. For example, in the San Diego area, farmers who obtain water from the federal government pay as little as $2.50 for an acre-foot of water (326,000 gallons). A city resident, on the other hand, pays $300 for the same amount.

Conservationists are trying to find ways to help the California refuges. One approach is to buy water rights for them. That way, at least some water will come to the refuges even during a drought. Another approach is to pressure the government to charge farmers more for their water, forcing them to conserve it rather than use it thoughtlessly.

The water problem is even more serious at Stillwater National Wildlife Refuge in Nevada, one of the few wet areas in this desert state. Waterfowl have almost nowhere else to go to breed, rest, and feed. But water is in great demand for agriculture, and none was set aside for the refuge. As a result, Stillwater had been receiving only water returned from crop irrigation, which is often polluted. Now The Nature Conservancy is buying water rights for the refuge from farmers willing to sell them. At Stillwater, buying water rights is critical to waterfowl survival.

Refuges and the Military

During World War II, the United States military needed land for preparing its fighting men, and Congress gave it permission to use some wildlife refuges as training grounds. Ever since, wildlife on these refuges has had to cope with bombs dropping, tanks ripping up the ground, and jet planes roaring through the air. Military air exercises, considered by refuge managers to be especially harmful to wildlife, took place over at least 55 refuges in 1989 and continue to occur. During these exercises, weapons are tested, jet dogfights are staged, and bombs are dropped—all accompanied by ground-shaking sonic booms, often more than a dozen each day.

Unfortunately, the U.S. Fish and Wildlife Service can do little, because it shares jurisdiction of these refuges with the Department of Defense. Refuge managers can negotiate conditions with the military in order to minimize the impact on wildlife, but military trainees sometimes ignore them completely. At Desert Refuge in Nevada, for example, military planes frequently fly as low as 100 feet above the ground, even though the minimum required altitude, except under exceptional circumstances, is 2,000 feet. Bombs are dropped on two valleys in the refuge. The largest population of the desert bighorn sheep lives on Desert Refuge, and refuge officials believe that such loud and persistent military activity disturbs the lives of the sheep significantly. The endangered desert tortoise makes its home there as well. Yet Congress renewed the law allowing the military to use the refuge in the mid-1980s, and the law does not come up for consideration again until the beginning of the twenty-first century.

Refuges for Private Gain

Perhaps the most frustrating problem for the Refuge System is private rights to use these public lands. Such privileges come about in a variety of ways. One way is when a company owns the mineral rights on a refuge. Then it can mine there, and there is little the government can do about it. Fortunately, some companies are willing to work with refuge management to reduce the impact of their activities. Even so, mining was second only to military air exercises in activities that refuge managers considered harmful in 1989. Logging is also allowed on some refuges. Both mining and logging dam-

Logging, which occurs on some refuges, destroys homes for birds like this short-eared owl.

age the landscape in serious ways, eliminating habitat for just those animals the refuges are supposed to be helping. But even on refuges where the government has control, pressure from industry can be intense, as when oil companies wanted to drill on the Arctic National Wildlife Refuge in Alaska, a critical caribou breeding area.

Some refuge lands are not even owned by the government. Rather, they are "easements" granted by property owners, usually farmers. The easements provide restrictions on hunting, public entry, and/or draining of wetlands. But on such refuges, any activity can take place that is not specifically forbidden by the easement. Farmers often continue raising crops, haying, and livestock grazing, all of which can be harmful to wildlife. Farming seriously alters habitat. Crop plants replace native vegetation, and harvesting of crops disturbs the landscape. When livestock like cattle are allowed to graze on a refuge, they compete with wildlife for food. In addition, cattle can contaminate ponds and creeks with their manure when they retreat to the coolness of a shady streamside on a hot day.

Cattle like these can damage wildlife habitat when they graze on refuges.

·5·

Refuges in the Future

*A*s the one hundredth anniversary of the National Wildlife Refuge System approaches, the U.S. Fish and Wildlife Service is examining refuge goals and activities closely. As part of its Refuge 2003 program, meetings were held around the country in 1991 to find out what citizens wanted from their refuges. Citizens were also encouraged to write letters expressing their feelings about appropriate activities on the refuges. The results of this public input will be incorporated into future refuge management policies, making the System more responsive to the desires of the American people. And all along, new lands and water are being added to the System, increasing areas that provide protection and habitat improvement for wild plants and animals.

Red Rocks National Wildlife Refuge in Montana.

Solving Problems

Since the refuges are set aside for the benefit of wildlife, managers are not supposed to allow secondary uses that are harmful to the native plants and animals. But they don't always have a choice. The manager may be pressured by his or her superiors, who in turn are pressured by Congress or special interest groups, to allow certain activities to take place.

Local special interests also can be so strong that they are hard to resist. For example, by 1988, the beaches at Chincoteague had become so popular that local businesses looked upon them as a great tourist attraction. When tourists come, they spend money. The business community feared that closing the beaches would hurt the local economy. This concern made the decision to close part of the beach very controversial.

While refuge managers will always have to find ways of living in peace with local people, pressure from special interest groups would be easier to resist if the managers knew that

Wild animals like bighorn sheep find homes on western wildlife refuges.

their efforts to fulfill the purpose of their refuges—management primarily for the benefit of wildlife—were completely supported by the Congress in Washington and by the American people.

Resisting outside pressure is also easier when a refuge has a clearly defined legal purpose such as providing habitat for waterfowl or protecting a particular endangered species. But some refuges lack a clear statement of purpose, making it difficult to decide whether a secondary use conflicts. The refuges whose legal purposes haven't been properly defined need to be studied and clarified.

The controversies over refuge problems may seem discouraging. But in the long run, knowledge of problems can lead to solutions. In addition to the U.S. Fish and Wildlife Service's public Refuge 2003 program, a variety of conservation organizations have been investigating the Refuge System, pinpointing problems, and suggesting solutions.

In 1988, The Wilderness Society published a report called "Ten Most Endangered National Wildlife Refuges," which spells out problems at refuges and recommends solutions.

Defenders of Wildlife is also focusing on the Refuge System, recommending that the System's role in protecting biological diversity and helping endangered species be strengthened. The private National Wildlife Refuge Association provides members with important information about refuges. In addition, the National Wildlife Federation has also helped bring the problems of our refuges to public attention.

Wildlife viewing, when done with respect for the animals, is a healthy human activity on refuges.

The endangered Hawaiian stilt finds a home on the Hanalei National Wildlife Refuge in Hawaii. Photo by Dorothy H. Patent.

The Next Century

In our crowded world, humans must work actively to protect the wildlands where plants and animals make their homes. There are many ways individual people can help out. Letters to congressmen supporting conservation provide pressure in the right direction. In addition, many refuges welcome volunteers of all ages who can help in a variety of ways such as banding waterfowl or leading nature hikes.

We have changed the earth to meet our material needs, and now we have a responsibility to the rest of the living world and to the human spirit. Without careful planning and hard choices, other living things will lose out, and Earth will become a sadder, less healthy planet. As we destroy wild habitat, we also harm ourselves, for we are a part of nature. We need wild places to refresh our spirits, and we require clean air, land, and water for our own survival.

We hear so much about the destruction of the tropical rainforests that we sometimes forget that habitat for wild creatures is disappearing on our own doorstep as well. As the only federal lands that are meant to be managed primarily for the benefit of wildlife, the National Wildlife Refuge System is a good place to focus attention on conserving homes for wild things.

White-tailed deer.

Sunlight reflects off the canopy of leaves in a forest.

Where to Write for More Information about National Wildlife Refuges

Defenders of Wildlife
1244 Nineteenth Street, N.W.
Washington, D.C. 20036

The Nature Conservancy
1815 North Lynn Street
Arlington, VA 22209

National Wildlife Federation
8925 Leesburg Pike
Vienna, VA 22184

The Wilderness Society
900 Seventeenth Street, N.W.
Washington, D.C. 20006-2596

National Wildlife Refuge
   Association
10824 Fox Hunt Lane
Potomac, MD 20854

U.S. Fish and Wildlife Service
   Division of Refuges, Room 670
4401 North Fairfax Drive
Arlington, VA 22203

Index

In this index, National Wildlife Refuge is abbreviated NWR.

Agassiz NWR, 19
Animals, 12, 31, 35–38, 51–53, 56–59, 61, 66. *See also* Birds
Antioch Dunes NWR, 15–16, 41–44
Aransas NWR, 15, 16, 40
Arctic NWR, 67

Birds, 11–15, 30–31, 33–34, 37–39, 44–50, 54–56, 59, 62–64; migration of, 14–15
Bison, 11, 12, 13, 59
Bitterroot National Forest, 24
Bosque del Apache NWR, 20, 25, 27–33
Buckwheat, 43
Bull's Island, 33–34
Bureau of Land Management, 24
Bureau of Reclamation, 24
Butterflies, 16, 42–43

Cape Romain NWR, 33–36
Central Valley (CA), 59–65
Chincoteague NWR, 54

Deer, 19, 20, 56–59
Defenders of Wildlife, 26, 73
Department of Defense, 24, 66
Des Lacs NWR, 17
Desert National Wildlife Range, 17
Desert Refuge, 66
Diversity, preservation of, 16

Duck Stamp Law, 12–14, 55
Ducks, 48–50, 55–56. *See also* Birds

Easements, 67–68
Education, environmental, 20, 39

Farallon NWR, 27
Farming, 25, 33, 62–65, 68

Glacier National Park, 22
Grays Lake NWR, 30
Grazing, 20, 68

Hanalei NWR, 74
Havasu NWR, 17
Hunting, 12–14, 19, 22, 33, 55–59, 68

Iroquois NWR, 39
Irrigation. *See* Water resources

Kenai NWR, 18
Kesterton NWR, 62
Kilauea Point NWR, 21

Lee Metcalf NWR, 48, 61
Logging, 20, 22, 24, 25, 66

McFadden NWR, 12
Mining, 20, 22, 25, 66

National Bison Range, 11–13, 59, 61
National forests, 22, 24
National Park Service, 22
National parks, 22
National Resource Lands, 24
National Wildlife Federation, 73
National Wildlife Refuge
    Association, 73
National Wildlife Refuge System:
    founding of, 11; future of, 69–75
Nature Conservancy, 65
Ninepipe NWR, 50, 52

Oil drilling, 67
Okefenokee NWR, 17

Pacific Gas & Electric Co., 42
Pelican Island, 11
Pelicans, 34
Plants, 16, 37, 43–45, 68
Prairie pothole region, 19, 46–47
Public lands, 22–25

Recreation, 19–20, 22, 51–55
Red Rocks NWR, 70
Refuge 2003 program, 69, 73
Refuges: location of, 8–9, 14–17;
    military use of, 65–66; private
    use of, 20, 25, 66–68; public use
of, 19–20, 27, 51–59, 68; purposes
    of, 12, 14–16, 18–20, 25–26, 69–75
Rookeries, 34
Roosevelt, Theodore, 11

Salton Sea NWR, 17
San Francisco Bay NWR, 20, 36–39
Sandhill cranes, 30–31
Selenium, 62
Squaw Creek NWR, 15
Stillwater NWR, 65

"Ten Most Endangered National
    Wildlife Refuges," 73
Tinicum National Environmental
    Center, 20, 22
Turtles, 35–36, 66

U.S. Fish and Wildlife Service, 12,
    20, 42, 66
U.S. Forest Service, 22

Water resources, 19, 24, 25, 31, 47,
    59–65
Waterfowl. See Birds; Ducks
Wetlands, 13–14, 37, 47–48, 61–62,
    68
Whooping cranes, 15, 30–31, 33
Wichita Mountains NWR, 12
Wilderness areas, 24–25
Wilderness Society, 26, 73